# FUN TO WEAR AND GREAT TO SHARE!

**FUN TO WEAR AND GREAT TO SHARE!** Our 48 fabulous friend they're cool! These trendy wrist wraps can show your team sp or remind best buds that you think they're totally awesome! J knot colorful embroidery floss into amazing armbands. We've even included skill-level symbols so you'll know which ones take more time and experience.

◯ Super Simple  ▢ On Your Way  ✡ Challenger

Whether you go wild or keep it mild, your choices of style, colors, beads, and charms will make each bracelet one-of-a-kind.
Have fun!

## READ THIS FIRST!

◆ Leave 3" to 4" of thread at both ends to tie around your wrist.

◆ Support threads are threads around which some knots are made. They must be taut as you work. Wrap the tail end around your shirt button or fasten with a pin.

◆ Tie knots with an upward motion.

◆ Tape start to something steady like a tabletop, a clipboard, or pin to your jeans.

◆ On Square Knots, Right Knots, & Left Knots remember to always tie twice.

## 3 Color Abstract Chevron Single

### Colors: A-blue, B-cream, & C-peach

1. You will need to cut three 36" lengths of A & B & two 36" lengths of C.

2. Tie together & tape down in this order.

AA A B B B C C

3. On the left side, make a left knot with A onto A (remember to tie twice). Repeat knot with A onto next A, then with A onto B. You have made 3 left knots.

4. On the right side, make a right knot with C onto C (remember to tie twice). Repeat knot with C onto B, then with C onto next B. You have made 3 right knots.

5. Knots will form a V when you now make a right knot with C onto A.

6. Repeat knots - always working toward center with outside threads.

7. When bracelet is the right length, tie a knot & trim.

## Scrap Spiral

### Colors: peach, green, blue, & brown

1. You will need to cut four or five 2-yard lengths of any remaining colors. If some are too short, tie them together to make a longer thread - the knot will not show when you are finished. You can combine colors.

2. Double threads, tie a knot, & tape down. Color order does not matter.

3. Take a double strand of one color & make left knots around the remaining threads.

4. Change the color you are tying with after 1 knot, 2 knots, or just whenever you feel like it.

5. Knot, using left knots all the way, until bracelet is the right length. Tie a knot & trim.

©1999 by Leisure Arts, Inc., 5701 Ranch Drive, Little Rock, AR 72223-9633   ISBN 1-57486-662-1

 PRINTED WITH SOY INK

 Made in U.S.A.

1

## 4 Color Triple Square Knot Double with Beads

## Narrow 5 Color Chevron Single

### Colors: A-light purple, B-dark pink, C-light pink, & D-white

**1** You will need to cut four 36" lengths each of A, B, & C & three 36" lengths of D. You will also need 30 beads.

**2** Double each D thread. Tie together in 3 bundles - 4 As + 1 doubled D, 4 Bs + 1 doubled D, 4 Cs + 1 doubled D. Then tie all 3 together & tape down in this order. In this design you use 2 threads together like a single thread.

**3** Put 10 beads onto each doubled support thread (D). Fasten the support threads from each group separately to your shirt - put beads close to you.

**4** First in A section, then in C section, make 1 square knot around support threads (remember to tie twice).

**5** In B section make 3 square knots around support thread.

**6** In A & C sections slide down 1 bead, then make a square knot under each bead.

**7** Take right threads from A & left threads from B & make a square knot. Repeat with left threads from C & right threads from B.

**8** In the B section slide down a bead & make a square knot under the bead. You have now joined all 3 color sections - & added beads!

**9** Repeat steps 4-8 until bracelet is the right length.

**10** Tie a knot in each color section, then tie the 3 sections together. Trim.

### Colors: A-pink, B-light green, C-white, D-green, & E-purple

**1** You will need to cut one 36" length of each color.

**2** Tie together & tape down in this order.

**3** Make a left knot with A onto B (remember to tie twice). Repeat with A onto C.

**4** Make a right knot with E onto D (remember to tie twice).

**5** Knots will form a V when you now make a right knot in the center with E onto C.

**6** Repeat knots, always working toward the center with your outside threads.

**7** When the length is right, tie a knot & trim.

2

## 3 Color Half Square Twist with Beads

### Colors: A-light pink, B-dark pink, & C-white

1. You will need to cut one 36" length each of A & B & two 18" lengths of C. You will also need 8 beads.

2. Tie together & tape down in this order.

3. Using your 2 support threads (C) like a single thread, put the beads on the threads. Fasten the ends of the support threads to your shirt - put beads close to you.

4. Tie ½ of a square knot. Pull up tight - but not too tight.

5. Tie 5 of the ½ square knots & then slide down a bead.

6. Tie next ½ square knot under the bead.

7. Repeat steps 5 & 6 until the length is right. Tie a knot & trim.

## 5 Color Diagonal Single

### Colors: A-white, B-pink, C-green, D-purple, & E-light green

1. You will need to cut two 36" lengths of each color.

2. Tie together & tape down in this order.

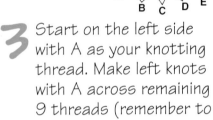

3. Start on the left side with A as your knotting thread. Make left knots with A across remaining 9 threads (remember to tie twice).

4. Start again on the left side & make left knots across with the other A.

5. Repeat knots - always starting with the left thread & working left to right. A diagonal pattern will form.

6. Work until the length is right. Tie a knot & trim.

## 2 Color Half Square Twist With Charms

### Colors: A-dark pink, B-light pink, & C-white

1. You will need to cut two 72" lengths each of A & B & two 20" lengths of C. You will also need 2 charms.

2. Put 1 charm on the A threads & the other on the B threads. Fold the A & B threads so they are doubled &, with the charms in the folds, tie all threads together & tape down in this order. Fasten the other ends of the support threads (C) to your shirt. In this design you use 4 threads together like a single thread.

3. Make ½ of a square knot around your support threads. Pull up tight - but not too tight.

4. Work until the length is right. Tie a knot & trim.

# 4 Color Zig-Zag Diagonal

## Colors: A-purple, B-green, C-yellow, & D-blue

1 You will need to cut two 36" lengths of each color.

2 Tie together & tape down in this order.

A A B B C C D D

3 Start on the left side with A as your knotting thread. Make left knots with A across remaining threads (remember to tie twice).

4 Start again on left side & make left knots across with the other A.

5 Repeat knots - always starting with the left thread. Work left to right. A diagonal pattern will form.

6 Knot 8 rows - 2 rows of each color. Untape, turn over, & tape down again.

7 Knot another 8 rows in reverse color order - D, C, B, A.

8 Turn over & repeat steps 6 & 7.

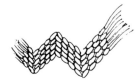

9 Work until the length is right. Tie a knot & trim.

# Square Knot Double with Beads

## Color: A & B-blue

1 You will need to cut four 36" lengths (A) & two 18" lengths (B). You will also need 8 beads.

2 Tie together & tape down in this order. In this design you use 2 threads together like a single thread.

A A B B A A

3 Put the beads onto your support threads (B). Put beads close to you. Fasten the other end of your support threads to your shirt.

4 Make 4 square knots with double outside threads (remember to tie twice).

5 Slide down 1 bead & make 1 square knot under the bead.

6 Slide down 1 bead & make 4 or 5 square knots.

7 Repeat steps 5 & 6 until the length is right. Tie a knot & trim.

## 4 Color Double Diagonal

### Colors: A-pink, B-purple, C-green, & D-black

1. You will need to cut two 36" lengths of each color.

2. Tie together & tape down in this order. In this design you use 2 threads together like a single thread.

3. Start on the left side with double As as your knotting thread. Make left knots across remaining thread pairs (remember to tie twice).

4. Start again on left side & make left knots across with B.

5. Repeat knots - always starting with the left threads. Work left to right. A diagonal pattern will form.

6. Work until bracelet is the right length. Tie a knot & trim.

## Reversible Square Knot Single

### Colors: A-green, B-purple, & C-white

1. You will need to cut one 38" length each of A & B & two 18" lengths of C.

2. Tie together & tape down in this order.

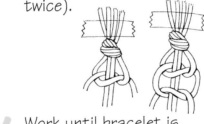

3. Make square knots using outside threads (remember to tie twice).

4. Work until bracelet is the right length. Tie a knot & trim.

## Basic Left Knot

### Colors: orange, blue, 2 purples, red, black, green, & white

1. You will need to cut 36" lengths of 4, 6, or 8 colors.

2. Tie together and tape down in any order.

3. Divide threads into 2 groups & make left knots all the way down.

4. Work until the length is right. Tie a knot & trim.

## 2 Color Chevron Christmas

### Colors: A-silver & B-metallic blue

1. You will need to cut two 72" lengths of A & one 72" length of B. You will also need 3 charms.

2. Put a charm onto each thread. Fold the threads so they are doubled &, with the charms in the fold, tie all threads together & tape down in this order.

3. Make a left knot with A onto A (remember to tie twice). Repeat with A onto B.

4. Make a right knot with A onto A (remember to tie twice). Repeat with A onto B.

5. Knots will form a V when you now make a right knot in the center with A onto A.

6. Always working toward the center with your outside threads, repeat knots until the length is right. Tie a knot & trim.

Keep your tension even; try to finish a bracelet in one sitting so that it will have a consistent tension.

## Slim Square Knot Double with Beads

### Colors: A-orange & B-black

**1** You will need to cut four 30" lengths of A & one 20" length of B. You will also need 5 beads.

**2** Tie together & tape down in this order.

**3** Put the beads onto your support thread (B). Fasten the other end of the support thread to your shirt - put beads close to you.

A B A

**4** Make 8 square knots with double outside threads (remember to tie twice).

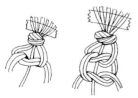

**5** Slide down 1 bead & make 4 more square knots (make certain the first knot under the bead is tight to the bead-this makes a "right side" to the bracelet with threads stranded tightly across the wrong side).

**6** Repeat step 5 until bracelet is right length, ending with 8 square knots.

**7** Tie a knot & trim.

## 3 Color Woven

### Colors: A-orange, B-blue, & C-pink

**1** You will need to cut two 20" lengths of A & four 20" lengths each of B & C.

**2** Separate into 5 pairs - same colors together. Tie together & tape down in this order. In this design you use 2 threads together like a single thread.

C C V V V
C B C B A

**3** Start on the right side with your 2 outside A threads & weave toward the left. Hold the remaining threads tightly & pull up on your A weaving strands. They should be right next to the knot above.

**4** Start again on the right side with your outside B threads.

**5** Continue weaving from right to left, pulling weaving threads up tightly, until bracelet is the right length.

**6** Tie a knot & trim.

## 4 Color Abstract Chevron Double

### Colors: A-red, B-orange, C-purple, & D-black

**1** You will need to cut four 36" lengths each of A & B & two 36" lengths each of C & D.

**2** Tie together & tape down in this order. In this design you use 2 threads together like a single thread.

V V V V V
A B C D B A

**3** On the left side, make a left knot with A onto B (remember to tie twice). Repeat knot with A onto C.

**4** On the right side, make a right knot with A onto B (remember to tie twice). Repeat knot with A onto D.

**5** Knots will form a V when you now make a right knot with A onto A in the center.

**6** Repeat until bracelet is the right length, always working toward the center with your outside threads. Tie a knot & trim.

## 5 Color Twist & Twist

### Colors: red, green, purple, orange, & blue

**1** You will need to cut one 36" length of each color.

**2** Tape down securely - in any order & without knotting.

**3** Hold the other ends of all threads & twist them together....keep on twisting....& twisting....

**4** Carefully untape the start end. Hold both ends together. Instantly you have a twisted bracelet!

**5** Tie both ends together & the twist is permanent. For a tighter or looser twist, don't tie together, & do it again.

idea

Try different color, bead, and charm combinations.

7

## Double Square Knot Double with Beads

**Colors: A-red, B-light pink, & C-dark pink**

**1** You will need to cut four 84" lengths each of A & B & two 48" lengths of C. You will also need 10 beads.

**2** Put 1 bead onto each of the 10 threads.

**3** Fold all threads double. Tie together 2" below the beads & tape down in this order.

A   C   B

**4** In this design you tie knots around 2 pairs of support threads (C). Fasten the 2 support thread pairs a little bit apart from each other on your shirt.

**5** Using 4 A threads on each side, tie a square knot around the left support thread pair (remember to tie twice).

**6** Using 4 B threads on each side, tie a square knot around the right support thread pair.

**7** Now tie a square knot in the middle, using the 4 closest threads from each side. (This square knot has no support thread.)

**8** Repeat knots until you have 5" knotted.

**9** Divide remaining threads into 2 sections & braid each section until the bracelet length is right for you.

**10** Tie each braid with a knot, trim, & you have a new bracelet! You can slip the bead tassel through the braid loop to fasten - or tie.

8

# 3 Color Chevron Single

## Colors: A-pink, B-white, & C-green

1. You will need to cut four 36" lengths of A, two 36" lengths of B, & two 36" lengths of C.

2. Tie together & tape down in this order.

3. On the left side, make a left knot with A onto A (remember to tie twice). Repeat knot with A onto B, then with A onto C.

4. On the right side, make a right knot with A onto A (remember to tie twice). Repeat knot with A onto C, then with A onto B.

5. Now make a right knot in the center with A onto A & the V will form.

6. Repeat, always working with the outside threads to the center, until the bracelet is the right length. Tie a knot & trim.

# 5 Color Abstract Chevron Single

## Colors: A-red, B-light pink, C-dark pink, D-orange, & E-purple

1. You will need to cut two 36" lengths of each color.

2. Tie together & tape down in this order.

3. Make a left knot with A onto A (remember to tie twice), then onto B, B, & C. You have made 4 left knots.

4. On the right side, make a right knot with E onto E (remember to tie twice), then onto D, D, & C. You have made 4 right knots.

5. Knots will form a V when you now make a right knot with E onto A.

6. Repeat knots - always working toward the center with your outside threads- until the length is right. Tie a knot & trim.

# 3 Color Single Spiral

## Colors: A-red, B-light pink, & C-dark pink

1. You will need to cut one 36" length of each color.

2. Tie a knot & tape down in this order.

3. Make a left knot with the A thread around the 2 remaining threads, which act as support threads. Holding the support threads taut, tighten the knot with an upward motion.

4. Repeat step 3 for 1" then use B as your knotting thread. See the spiral!

5. Continue making left knots with 1 thread around 2 remaining threads, changing the color you are working with every inch until the bracelet is the right length.

6. Tie a knot & trim.

idea:

Look for unusual buttons or beads for your bracelets.

## 2 Color Abstract Chevron Double

### Colors: A-purple & B-green

1. You will need to cut six 36" lengths of each color.

2. Tie together & tape down in this order. In this design you use 2 threads together like a single thread.

3. On the left side, make a left knot with 2 As onto 2 As (remember to tie twice). Repeat with 2 As onto the next 2 As.

4. On the right side, make a right knot with 2 Bs onto 2 Bs (remember to tie twice). Repeat with 2 Bs onto the next 2 Bs.

5. Knots will form a V when you now make a right knot in the center with 2 Bs onto 2 As.

6. Repeat knots - always working toward the center with your outside threads, until the length is right.

7. Tie a knot & trim.

## Half Square Twist Foursome with Beads

### Color: A & B- yellow

1. You will need to cut eight 36" lengths (A) & two 18" lengths (B). You will also need 6 beads.

2. Tie together & tape down in this order.

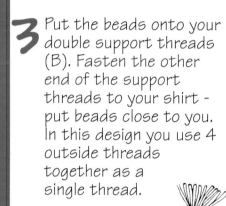

3. Put the beads onto your double support threads (B). Fasten the other end of the support threads to your shirt - put beads close to you. In this design you use 4 outside threads together as a single thread.

4. Make 1/2 of a square knot. Pull up tight - but not too tight or it will be stiff!

5. Make 4 of the 1/2 square knots & then slide down a bead.

6. Make next 1/2 square knot under the bead.

7. Repeat step 5 until the length is right. Tie a knot & trim.

## 3 Color Spaced Diagonal

### Colors: A-purple, B-green, & C-yellow

1. You will need to cut two 36" lengths of each color.

2. Tie together & tape down in this order.

3. Start on the left side with A as your knotting thread. Make left knots with A across remaining 5 threads (remember to tie twice).

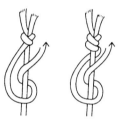

4. Start again on left side & make left knots across with the other A.

5. Repeat knots - always starting with the left thread. Work left to right. A diagonal pattern will form.

6. After 2 rows of each color, leave 1/2" unknotted space & start knotting again.

7. Repeat step 6 until the length is right. Tie a knot & trim.

## Spiral with Beads

### Color: A & B-purple

**1** You will need to cut one 40" length (A) & one 24" length (B). You will also need 4 beads.

**2** Thread the beads onto the support thread (B). Fold the support thread so that it is doubled. With the beads in the fold, knot all threads together & tape down.

**3** Use the long thread (A) to make left knots around the shorter threads. Holding support threads taut, tighten each knot with an upward motion— see the spiral!

**4** Work left knots until the bracelet is the right length. Tie a knot & trim.

## Slim Square Knot Double Message

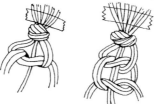

W W J D ?

### Color: A & B-yellow

**1** You will need to cut two 60" lengths (A) & one 20" length (B). You will also need one charm & 5 letter beads.

**2** Thread the charm onto the A threads. Double both A threads. With the charm in the fold, tie all threads together & tape down in this order. In this design you use 2 threads together like a single thread.

A A B A A

**3** Put the letter beads onto your support thread (B), taking care to thread them in the correct order to spell out your message.

**4** Make 14 square knots with double outside threads (remember to tie twice).

**5** Slide down 1 bead & make 1 more square knot.

**6** Repeat step 5 until all beads have been used. End with 14 square knots.

**7** Tie a knot & trim.

idea:

Remember...
Practice makes perfect!

11

## 5 Color Split Chevron

### Colors: A-white, B-peach, C-green, D-yellow, & E-rust

**1** You will need to cut two 36" lengths of each color.

**2** Tie together & tape down in this order.

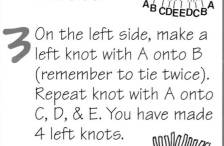

A B C D E E D C B A

**3** On the left side, make a left knot with A onto B (remember to tie twice). Repeat knot with A onto C, D, & E. You have made 4 left knots.

**4** On the right side, make a right knot with A onto B (remember to tie twice). Repeat knot with A onto C, D, & E. You have made 4 right knots.

**5** Start again on the left side & make 4 left knots with B. On the right side, make 4 right knots with B. Do not join in the center.

**6** You are working 2 separate sections, a right & a left. Every 10th row (every other E row) join the 2 sections by making a right knot with E onto E.

**7** When bracelet is the right length, join the sections with a knot & trim.

## Half & Half Double Diagonal

### Colors: A-yellow & B-brown

**1** You will need to cut five 36" lengths of each color.

**2** Double each bunch of color & loop together.

A

B

**3** Tie a ½ square knot with the A threads & another with the B threads.

A   B

**4** Tape down in the center. In this design you use 2 threads together like a single thread. You work the A end of the bracelet first and then the B end.

B

A

**5** Arrange your A threads in pairs. Start with the left A pair as your knotting thread. Make left knots across remaining 4 pairs (remember to tie twice).

**6** Repeat knots, always starting on the left, until you are 3" from the center ½ square knot. Tie a knot.

**7** Untape, turn around, & repeat steps 5 & 6 on the B side.

**8** Make a simple braid on each end until the bracelet is the right length.

**9** Tie a knot in each end & trim.

## 4 Color Twist & Twist

### Colors: rust, beige, green, & brown

**1** You will need to cut one 30" length of each color.

**2** Tape down securely - don't knot. Color order doesn't matter.

**3** Hold the other ends of all threads & twist them together....keep on twisting....& twisting....

**4** Carefully untape the start end. Hold both ends together. Instantly you have a twisted bracelet!

**5** Tie both ends together & the twist is permanent. For a tighter or looser twist, don't tie together & do it again.

## Reversible Square Knot Double

### Colors: A-cream, B-maroon, & C-brown

**1** You will need to cut two 40" lengths each of A & B & four 18" lengths of C.

**2** Tie together & tape down in this order.

**3** Make square knots using double outside threads (remember to tie twice). Each knot should lie tightly against the previous knot.

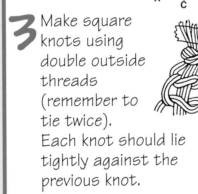

**4** Repeat knots until bracelet is the right length. Tie a knot & trim.

## Really Wide 4 Color Chevron Single

### Colors: A-cream, B-yellow, C-brown, & D-green

**1** You will need to cut four 36" lengths each of A, B, & C & two 36" lengths of D.

**2** Tie together & tape down in this order.

**3** On the left side, make a left knot with A onto A (remember to tie twice).

**4** Repeat knots with A across B threads, C threads & 1 D thread, a total of 6 left knots.

**5** On the right side, make 6 right knots with A (remember to tie twice).

**6** Knots will form a V when you now make a right knot in the center with A onto A.

**7** Repeat knots - always working toward the center with your outside threads.

**8** When bracelet is the right length, tie a knot & trim.

*idea:*

Pin or tie your support threads to your shirt; fasten the other end of the threads to a clipboard. Decorate the clipboard with paint and stickers.

### Colors: A-red, B-white, & C-blue (metallics)

**1** You will need to cut one 72" length of each color. You will also need 3 charms.

**2** Place a charm on each thread; fold the thread, doubling it. With the charms in the folds of the threads, leave a 3 - 4" length & tie a knot. Tape down the start end. In this design you use each doubled thread like a single thread.

**3** Make a left knot with A around the remaining threads, which act as support threads. Holding the support threads taut, tighten the knot with an upward motion.

**4** Repeat step 3 for 1" then change colors. See the spiral!

**5** Continue changing the color you are working with every inch until the bracelet is the right length. Tie a knot & trim.

### Color: A & B-white

**1** You will need to cut four 60" lengths (A) & two 18" lengths (B). You will also need 20 beads.

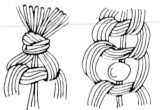

**2** Double the A threads. Tie all threads together & tape down in this order. Thread the beads onto your support threads (B). Fasten the ends of the support threads to your shirt - put beads close to you.

**3** Make 3 square knots with the 4 outside threads on each side (remember to tie twice).

**4** Slide down 4 beads. Make another 3 square knots below the bead.

**5** Repeat step 4 until bracelet is the right length, ending with 3 square knots. Tie a knot & trim.

14

## Square Knot Single with Beads

### Color: A & B-white

**1** You will need to cut two 36" lengths (A) & two 18" lengths (B). You will also need 3 patterned beads and 4 plain beads.

**2** Tie together & tape down in this order.

**3** Put the beads onto your support threads (B), alternating the type of bead. Fasten the other end of your support threads to your shirt - put beads close to you.

**4** Make a square knot with the 2 outside threads (remember to tie twice). Pull up tight - but not too tight!

**5** Make 4 square knots total & then slide down a bead. Make next square knot under the bead.

**6** Repeat step 5 until all beads have been used. End with 4 square knots. Tie a knot & trim.

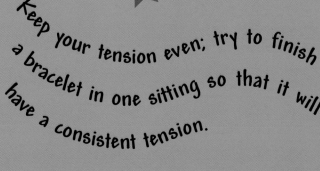
Keep your tension even; try to finish a bracelet in one sitting so that it will have a consistent tension.

## Spiral with Bead

### Color: A & B-red

**1** You will need to cut one 40" length (A) & three 12" lengths (B). You will also need 1 long bead.

**2** Tie together & tape down in this order.

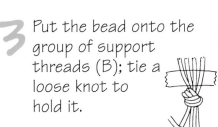

**3** Put the bead onto the group of support threads (B); tie a loose knot to hold it.

**4** Use your A thread to make a left knot around the support threads. Holding support threads taut, tighten each knot with an upward motion.

**5** Keep making left knots just below the previous knot - see how the spiral starts.

**6** When the bracelet is slightly less than half the length you want, slip up the bead - slide your knotting threads through - then continue knots.

**7** Work until the length is right. Tie a knot & trim.

## 4 Color Round Braid

### Colors: A-dark blue, B-medium blue, C-light blue, & D-white

**1** You will need to cut two 20" lengths of each color.

**2** Tie threads together & tape down in this order. In this design you use 2 threads together like a single thread.

**3** Knot like this. Pull up tightly.

**4** Repeat step 3 until bracelet is the right length. Tie a knot & trim.

## 5 Color Woven

### Colors: A-dark blue, B-white, C-pink, D-green, & E-light blue

**1** You will need to cut two 20" lengths of each color.

**2** Tie together & tape down in this order. In this design you use 2 threads together like a single thread.

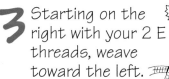

**3** Starting on the right with your 2 E threads, weave toward the left.

**4** Hold remaining threads tightly & pull up on your E weaving threads. They should be right next to the knot above.

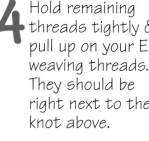
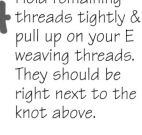

**5** Always starting with your right-hand threads, repeat steps 3 & 4 until bracelet is the right length. Tie a knot & trim.

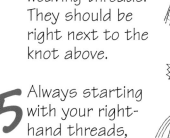

## Half Square Twist

### Color: A & B-green

**1** You will need to cut two 36" lengths (A) & two 20" lengths (B).

**2** Tie together & tape down in this order. Pin the support threads (B) to your shirt - do not untie until you're done or the twist will come out!

**3** Make ½ of a square knot. Pull up tight - but not too tight or it will be stiff.

**4** Repeat knots. Make certain each knot is lined up directly below previous knot. When bracelet is the right length, tie a knot & trim.

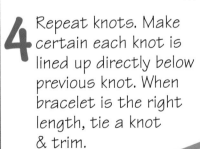

## Two Color Half Square Twist Double with Beads

### Colors: A & C-white B-blue

**1** You will need to cut two 36" lengths each of A & B & four 18" lengths of C. You will also need 3 beads.

**2** Tie together & tape down in this order. In this design you use 2 threads together like a single thread. Thread the beads onto your support threads (C)--tie the support threads to your shirt & put the beads close to you.

**3** Make twenty ½ square knots.

**4** Slide 1 bead down; make three ½ square knots.

**5** Repeat step 4 until all beads have been used. Finish the bracelet with twenty ½ square knots. Tie a knot & trim.

*For a beach-y bracelet, drill holes in small shells and tie those into your bracelet.*

## 3 Color Chevron Double

### Colors: A-green, B-pink, & C-purple

**1** You will need to cut four 36" lengths of each color.

**2** Tie together & tape down in this order. In this design you use 2 threads together like a single thread.

**3** Starting at the left, make a left knot with A onto B (remember to tie twice). Repeat with A onto C.

**4** On the right side, make a right knot with A onto B (remember to tie twice). Repeat knot with A onto C.

**5** Knots will form a V when you now make a right knot with A onto A.

**6** Repeat knots - always working toward the center with your outside threads.

**7** When bracelet is the right length, tie a knot & trim.

## 2 Color Half Square Twist

### Colors: A-black & B-white

1 You will need to cut one 36" length each of A & B & one 20" length each of A & B.

2 Tie together and tape down in this order with the 20" threads in the middle - these are your support threads.

A A B B

3 Make ½ of a square knot. Pull up tight - but not too tight or it will be stiff.

4 Repeat knots until bracelet is the right length. Tie a knot & trim.

## 3 Color Square Knot Double With Name

E M I L Y

### Colors: A-pink, B-green, & C-white

1 You will need to cut two 36" lengths each of A & B & one 20" length of C. You will also need desired letter beads.

2 Tie together and tape down in this order .

3 Put the beads onto your support thread (C), taking care to put them in the correct order for the name you want. Fasten the end of the support thread to your shirt & put the beads close to you. In this design you use 2 threads together like a single thread.

A A C B B

4 Make 12 square knots (remember to tie twice).

5 Slide down 1 bead. Make 2 more square knots.

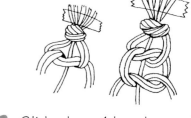

6 Repeat step 5 until the name is complete. Our name is five letters--for a longer or shorter name, you will need to adjust the number of knots between beads. End with 12 square knots. Tie a knot & trim.

## 2 Color Round Braid

### Colors: A-black & B-purple

1. You will need to cut four 20" lengths each of A & B.

2. Tie threads together & tape down in this order. In this design you use 2 threads together like a single thread.
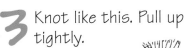
A A B B

3. Knot like this. Pull up tightly.
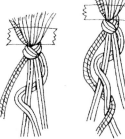

4. Repeat step 3 until bracelet is the right length. Tie a knot & trim.

## Double Spiral with Beads

### Color: A & B-black

1. You will need to cut two 36" lengths (A) & two 18" lengths (B). You will also need 5 beads.

2. Tie together & tape down in this order. In this design you use 2 threads together like a single thread. Put 5 beads onto your support threads (B) - attach the support threads to your shirt & put the beads close to you.
A A B B

3. Using the A threads, make 20 left knots.

4. Slide down 1 bead & make 8 left knots.

5. Repeat step 4 until all beads have been used. Finish with 20 left knots.

6. Tie a knot & trim.

## 5 Color Spaced Diagonal Single

### Colors: A-black, B-dark purple, C-purple, D-light purple, & E-white

1. You will need to cut two 36" lengths each of A, B, C, & D & one 36" length of E.

2. Tie together & tape down in this order.
A B C D E D C B A

3. Start on the left side with A as your knotting thread. Make left knots with A across remaining 8 threads (remember to tie twice).

4. Start again on the left side & make left knots across with B. Repeat knots - always starting with the left thread. A diagonal pattern will form.

5. After 5 rows, leave about 1/2" unknotted space & then start knotting again.

6. Repeat 5 row - space pattern until the bracelet is the right length. Tie a knot & trim.

*idea:* Make sure you leave enough floss at the end of the bracelet to tie it onto your wrist!

## Double Half Square Twist with Beads

### Color: A & B-black

**1** You will need to cut four 36" lengths (A) & two 20" lengths (B). You will also need 3 beads.

**2** Take 3 threads & tie a large knot at the end of each thread. Put 1 bead onto each of these threads - slide beads down to the knots. Tie all threads together 3-4" from the beads. Tape down in this order. In this design you will use 2 threads together like a single thread.

**3** Make ½ of a square knot around your support threads (B). Pull up tight - but not too tight or it will be stiff.

**4** Repeat knots until bracelet is the right length. Tie a knot & trim.

## Wide 5 Color Chevron Single

### Colors: A-medium green, B-white, C-light green, D-dark green, & E-black

**1** You will need to cut two 36" lengths of each color.

**2** Tie together & tape down in this order.

**3** On the left side, make a left knot with A onto B (remember to tie twice). Repeat knots with A onto C, D, & E.

**4** On the right side, make a right knot with A onto B. Repeat knots with A onto C, D, & E.

**5** Knots will form a V when you now make a right knot with A onto A.

**6** Always working toward the center with your outside threads, repeat knots until the length is right. Tie a knot & trim.

## 2 Color Abstract Chevron Single

### Colors: A-white & B-black

**1** You will need to cut two 36" lengths of A & three 36" lengths of B.

**2** Tie together & tape down in this order.

**3** On the left side, make a left knot with B onto B (remember to tie twice). Repeat with B onto B.

**4** On the right side, make a right knot with A onto A (remember to tie twice).

**5** Knots will form a V when you now make a right knot in the center with A onto B.

**6** Always working toward the center with your outside threads, repeat knots until the length is right. Tie a knot & trim.

Production Team-Technical: Heather Doyal. Art: John Rose and Mark Potter Editorial: Hope Turner. Instructions tested by: E. Brooke Bennett.